D1305486

Marshall Co Public Library
@ Benton
1003 Poplar Street
Benton, KY 42025

Garrett Book Company

FEB 18 2011

The FBI and Crimes Against Children

By Sabrina Crewe

MASON CREST PUBLISHERS

Produced in association with Water Buffalo Books.
Design by Westgraphix LLC.

Copyright © 2010 by Mason Crest Publishers. All rights reserved. No part of this publication may be reproduced or transmitted in any form or by any means, electronic or mechanical, including photocopying, recording, taping, or any information storage and retrieval system, without permission from the publisher.

MASON CREST PUBLISHERS INC.
370 Reed Road
Broomall, Pennsylvania 19008
(866) MCP-BOOK (toll free)
www.masoncrest.com

Printed in the United States of America

First Printing

9 8 7 6 5 4 3 2 1

Library of Congress Cataloging-in-Publication Data

Crewe, Sabrina.
      The FBI and crimes against children / Sabrina Crewe.
         p. cm. — (The FBI story)
      Includes bibliographical references and index.
      ISBN 978-1-4222-0570-9 (hardcover) — ISBN 978-1-4222-1369-8 (pbk.)
  1. United States. Federal Bureau of Investigation—Juvenile literature. 2. Children—Crimes against—United States—Juvenile literature. 3. Criminal investigation—United States—Juvenile literature. I. Title.
    HV6250.4.C48C74 2009
    363.25'950830973—dc22   2008046344

Photo credits: © AP/Wide World Photos: cover (lower left, lower right, top right), 4, 6, 7, 8, 9, 12, 14, 19, 20, 24, 26, 28 (both), 29, 30 (both), 35, 39, 41, 42, 49, 51, 54; © Courtesy of FBI: 1, 5, 16, 17, 25, 34, 45, 46, 48, 57, 60 (left); © Getty Images: cover (top left), 37, 44, 53; © iStock Photos: 10 (both), 31, 55; Used under license from Shutterstock Inc.: cover (bottom center), 11, 13, 22, 60 (right).

Publisher's note:
All quotations in this book come from original sources and contain the spelling and grammatical inconsistencies of the original text.

CONTENTS

1 One Lost, Two Found

On January 8, 2007, Ben Ownby was on his way home from school in Beaufort, Missouri. He got off the bus at his usual stop on a rural road near his house. Then he disappeared.

Ben Ownby and his father, William "Don" Ownby, speak to reporters from their living room on January 16, 2007. By following up on leads in the immediate aftermath of Ben's kidnapping on January 8, FBI agents and other law enforcement officials were able to find Ben within days of his abduction.

Looking for Ben

Ben's parents reported him missing, and the hunt began. Volunteers combed the woods in the area around Ben's home. TV, radio, and newspaper reporters covered their search every step of the way. Law officers followed up on every lead. But there was no sign of Ben.

Some law officers involved in the case were agents from the Federal Bureau of Investigation (FBI). The FBI has special teams to deal with crimes against children. Part of their work involves investigating cases of **abduction**, or kidnapping.

When Ben was reported missing, the FBI's Child Abduction Rapid Deployment (CARD) team went to work. CARD investigators know that the first few hours of a kidnapping are vital. The FBI set up a command post for its own agents and other law officers. Hundreds of possible leads came into the command post to be processed.

The Crucial Lead

A crucial piece of information put investigators on the right track during those first few hours. Fifteen-year-old Mitchell Hults, who got off the school bus with Ben, described a white truck he had seen nearby. The truck's details were

FEDERAL BUREAU OF INVESTIGATION
CARD TEAM
CHILD ABDUCTION RAPID DEPLOYMENT

The emblem of the FBI's CARD teams conveys the sense of urgency in identifying and responding to child kidnappings as quickly as possible.

Michael Devlin is escorted out of a police van in Union, Missouri, during his trial in October 2007. Devlin was convicted and sentenced to life in prison on numerous charges related to the abductions of Shawn Hornbeck and Ben Ownby.

quickly distributed to police departments around the country. They were also broadcast on TV.

On January 11, 2007, two police officers spotted a truck matching the description outside an apartment in Kirkwood, Missouri. That night, officials arrived to question Michael Devlin, who lived in the apartment. A 15-year-old boy answered the door—it was not Ben. Both the boy and Devlin answered questions, but Devlin refused to let the officials inside.

End of the Ordeal

The next day, FBI agents and sheriff's deputies came back with a search warrant, which gave them the right to enter Devlin's home. There they found Ben Ownby and the boy who had answered the door. It turned out they had both been abducted and held by Devlin. So who was the other boy?

Eleven-year-old Shawn Hornbeck had last been seen riding his bicycle in Richwoods, Missouri, on October 6, 2002. Just like Ben, he had suddenly disappeared. Unlike Ben, however, he had been missing for more than four years. Shawn's parents lived in hope of finding him, but most people thought he was probably dead.

All that time, Shawn had been held by Michael Devlin. "What a blessing to find not one but two missing kids," said the FBI's Roland J. Corvington, agent in charge of the St. Louis, Missouri, office.

Shawn Hornbeck smiles at his stepfather, Craig Akers, on January 13, 2007. Shawn had been listed as missing since his kidnapping by Michael Devlin in October 2002. His rescue with Ben Ownby has been called the "Missouri Miracle."

SHAWN'S CAPTIVE YEARS

Shawn Hornbeck was riding his bicycle to a friend's house when he was abducted in 2002. Michael Devlin followed Shawn in his truck. He used a gun to threaten Shawn Hornbeck and force him into the truck. It was the first of many terrible ways Devlin kept Shawn under his control. For the first month, Shawn was tied up and gagged while Devlin was at work.

Every day, Devlin sexually abused Shawn. He planned to kill the boy a few weeks after kidnapping him. Devlin later confessed that he began to strangle Shawn, but Shawn talked him out of it. Shawn promised he would do whatever Devlin told him. And for more than four years, that is what happened. Shawn did not try to run away. He put up with horrible **abuse**.

Devlin took Shawn with him when he abducted Ben Ownby in 2007. He then made Shawn guard Ben while he went to work. According to FBI reports, Shawn tried to protect the younger boy from the worst of Devlin's abuse. Luckily, the hunt for Ben meant Shawn was finally rescued.

In 2008, one year after he was found, Shawn was catching up in school and had good grades. He was free once again to play baseball and basketball and ride his motorcycle. His family was trying to regain a normal life. As his stepfather said, however, "There's no way our lives will ever be the same as they were before Shawn's disappearance."

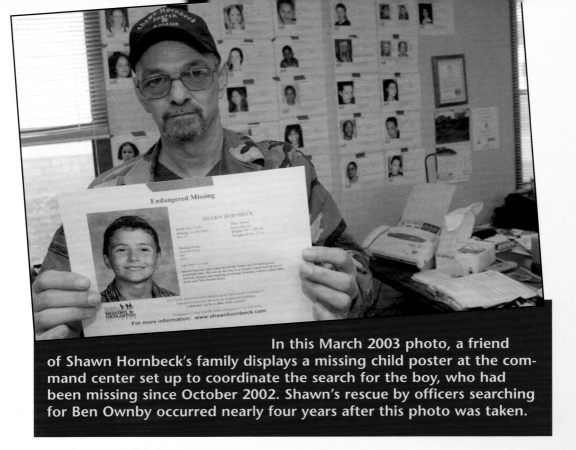

In this March 2003 photo, a friend of Shawn Hornbeck's family displays a missing child poster at the command center set up to coordinate the search for the boy, who had been missing since October 2002. Shawn's rescue by officers searching for Ben Ownby occurred nearly four years after this photo was taken.

Missing Children

Michael Devlin was sentenced to life in prison for kidnapping Ben Ownby and Shawn Hornbeck. He was also convicted of sexual abuse and of trying to kill Shawn.

In 2008, Ben's father, Don Ownby, was interviewed on NBC's *Today* show. He talked about life after the kidnapping. He said:

> You try not to worry. . . . You don't want him to have to worry about what's going on. It's just in the back of your mind all the time—"Where is he? Is he safe?"

Ben Ownby was only missing for a few days. Thousands of children, such as Shawn Hornbeck, stay missing for years, or forever. The FBI has hundreds of agents working to find missing children.

The Role of the FBI

The Federal Bureau of Investigation is the arm of the U.S. Department of Justice that investigates crimes all over the country. The FBI's job is to protect the nation and enforce national, or **federal**, laws.

FAST FACTS

As recently as 2005, 632,804 missing children were entered in the FBI's National Crime Information Center files. Most of them had not been abducted, and they were soon found.

FBI agents do this job by investigating crimes and by gathering information to prevent future crimes. The FBI's work covers many criminal activities. It includes everything from fraud to hate crimes. Agents investigate violent crimes, including some murders and gang violence.

Rachel Lloyd, head of Girls Education and Mentoring Service (GEMS), talks with one of the group's members. Lloyd is working to get states to follow federal guidelines in prosecuting adults who force children into **prostitution**. Most states treat child prostitutes as criminals and leave it up to the FBI and other federal agencies to prosecute the adults who force them into this form of slavery. GEMS is trying to get more states to treat child prostitutes as exploited victims, not criminals.

The Internet has given children a great opportunity to learn more and make new friends. Unfortunately, it has also made them easy targets for adults who would take advantage of them or abuse them.

The FBI investigates kidnappings and prostitution, often following criminals to foreign countries.

The FBI devotes great effort in fighting crimes that use computers and the Internet to harm children. In October 2003, President George W. Bush made remarks about children's online safety. In the course of his speech, he said:

> Our nation has made this commitment: Anyone who targets a child for harm will be a primary

target of law enforcement. That's our commitment. Anyone who takes the life or innocence of a child will be punished to the full extent of the law.

The FBI is very clear about its role in protecting children from violence and abuse. It tries to make children less **vulnerable** to sexual **exploitation**. Another goal is to respond rapidly to all crimes against children. The FBI also aims to help local law enforcers protect children by giving them support, training, and information.

As the families of Shawn Hornbeck and thousands of other abducted children know, a young boy or girl on a bicycle is a favorite target of adults who kidnap children. When kids are snatched off the streets, the FBI relies on people to come forward as witnesses as soon as possible to help the Bureau and other law enforcement agencies quickly identify, locate, and capture the kidnappers—and free the children.

2 Human Traffic: Child Prostitution and Slavery

The phrase "human trafficking" refers to an illicit trade in people, such as those who are sold as slaves or exploited in other ways. In the United States and many other countries, human trafficking is illegal. U.S. law also defines a related crime, "sex trafficking," which involves forcing or tricking

Officials applaud during the announcement in 2004 of a program intended to rescue young people who have been illegally detained and exploited by human traffickers. Other government programs aim at bringing traffickers to justice.

a person into becoming a worker in the sex trade (a prostitute). If that person is a child, the FBI's Crimes Against Children Unit gets involved. In most states in the United States, the legal definition of a child, or minor, includes anyone under the age of 18. In cases involving the use of alcohol, the term applies to anyone under 21.

Child workers, such as this boy in a **sweatshop** in India, are often tricked or forced into coming to the United States. Traffickers often keep child workers in a state of slavery by forcing them to work without pay.

Slave Labor

When Americans think of slavery, they probably have a mental picture of African Americans working on plantations hundreds of years ago. It's hard to believe that slavery still exists in the United States, but it does. People become slaves when their basic freedoms are taken away. Usually, they are held against their will and forced to work for no money.

Today, there are thousands of children from Central America and Asia who have been smuggled into the United States. They may have been bought or kidnapped in their home countries. But most of them have been tricked into coming. Traffickers promise good lives and good pay to the children and their parents.

Many young girls are forced to become domestic servants or sex workers. Boys may work in factories, fields, and restaurants. Why don't they escape? Usually, people who have been trafficked are scared. Traffickers threaten them and their families. Victims are beaten and abused. They are deprived of freedom and human contact. Most of them don't speak English or don't know where to go for help.

In 2005, the FBI began a Human Trafficking Initiative. Agents in FBI offices around the nation started working in their communities to fight trafficking. In 2007, the FBI's Civil Rights Unit opened 120 investigations into human

A member of Soroptimist International, an organization concerned with women's issues, hands out information in Philadelphia to increase awareness of human trafficking. Congress declared January 11 as the annual National Day of Human Trafficking Awareness in order to draw attention to the global crisis in the forced labor and sexual exploitation of children and adults alike.

trafficking. Agents arrested 155 people in connection with trafficking crimes.

Children in the Sex Trade

The FBI's Crimes Against Children unit focuses on the sex trade. Not all children who are victims of sex trafficking come from other countries. Many children exploited in the sex trade are U.S. citizens or residents. Often, they have run away from home. FBI Assistant Director Chris Swecker said in 2005 that "1.6 million children are estimated to run away from home each year, and [about] 40,000 of those children will have some type of . . . brush with sexual trafficking."

FAST FACTS

Human trafficking is a global business. The U.S. State Department estimates that two million people are trafficked worldwide every year.

The people who exploit children and others in the sex trade are known as pimps. A pimp usually has a few prostitutes, or sex workers, under his control. He forces them to hand over some or all of the money they earn. Some pimps find customers for their workers. Others send them to the streets to find their own customers. Many pimps use violence and threats to control sex workers. A 2005 article in *U.S. News and World Report* explains:

> Thousands of young girls and boys are falling victim to violent pimps, who move them from state to state, which makes it a federal matter. The younger they are, the more they are worth on the street.

CONNECTING THE DOTS

In December 2005, the FBI announced the end of a successful operation. "Precious Cargo" was an investigation into child sex trafficking. The investigation started in Harrisburg, Pennsylvania. Harrisburg was at the center of a prostitution ring. The FBI found that traffickers were taking women and girls to other states for prostitution. They were also selling and giving their victims to other traffickers to use as sex workers.

One person who worked on Precious Cargo was FBI intelligence analyst Jamie Konstas (pictured below in a publicity campaign by the FBI). Intelligence is the information gathered about a subject. Konstas's job was to gather and **analyze** (or study) intelligence relevant to the case. She collected thousands of toll records, which are lists of calls made to and from any telephone. Konstas was able to connect pimps in Harrisburg to traffickers in other places. The FBI and local law enforcement uncovered connections to other states, including Florida, Michigan, and Oklahoma.

"For cases involving child prostitution I connect the dots," explained Konstas in a 2006 interview. "It's not easy. Pimps travel a lot and use a number of aliases." But the work of Konstas, other experts, and the police led to many arrests. "The **evidence** we gathered exposed the massive scope of the prostitution ring," said Konstas.

Murder in Oklahoma City

In December 2002, a 14-year-old girl was murdered in Oklahoma City, Oklahoma. Her death was one of several among prostitutes who worked at truck stops in the area. FBI Special Agent Mike Beaver was the FBI coordinator for crimes against children in Oklahoma City. He wondered what the FBI could do to combat the violence. "The more we looked, the more we determined we needed to work child prostitution," he said.

Beaver's investigation uncovered a prostitution ring. The FBI found a network of pimps controlling more than 100 prostitutes, many of them underage (younger than 18). The network stretched into several states.

The FBI launched a nationwide effort to tackle child sex trafficking. The FBI's Innocence Lost project began in June 2003. The FBI's Innocence Lost team works with a child exploitation team in the Department of Justice and with the National Center for Missing and Exploited Children (NCMEC). Innocence Lost set up **task forces** in large cities where there were many underage sex workers.

The Attorney General's office issues an annual report on human trafficking. The 2007 report

The FBI's Innocence Lost team works with other groups to battle child sex trafficking.

showed that Innocence Lost has had good results. Between 2003 and 2007, Innocence Lost produced 365 investigations and 965 arrests. More than 350 children were found through the program.

FAST FACTS

The Department of Justice has a trafficking hotline. Victims of trafficking or those who suspect they know a victim can call 1-888-428-7581. People can report sexual exploitation of children on the National Center for Missing and Exploited Children CyberTipline: 1-800-843-5678.

Successful Sting

In June 2008, the FBI marked five years of Innocence Lost with a huge sting operation (a plan designed to catch criminals). First, the FBI identified organized networks across the nation that traffic children for sex. Then it planned Operation Cross Country.

The operation took five days and involved 350 law enforcement officers. Innocence Lost task forces in 16 cities swooped down on places where children worked in the sex trade. From Oakland, California, to Boston, Massachusetts, they went to truck stops, motels, and casinos. The FBI also targeted people using the Internet to advertise child sex workers. More than 350 people were arrested. Twenty-one children were rescued from traffickers.

3 Predators: The Internet and Child Porn

When children are kidnapped or abused, there are several ways to find the criminals and bring them to justice. Children are often able to identify their abusers, and investigators can use clues to trace their suspects. Sometimes, however, there are no physical clues.

The Cyber Criminal

The network of information we call the Internet is transmitted electronically into computers. Although the equipment used to send and receive Internet data is "hard" in the sense that it is tangible and can be turned on and off, the Internet itself exists largely in the form of digital codes and signals. That is why people call the Internet a "virtual" world.

An agent scans the contents of the hard drive of a computer. This computer was seized in a raid on a suspected child pornographer. Today, most child pornography is distributed over the Internet.

Forensics

19

A press conference in June 2008 announces an agreement among various Internet service providers to help state and federal agencies stop the spread of child pornography in cyberspace.

The term *virtual* refers to that which appears to be real but does not take up physical space. The virtual "world" of the Internet actually consists of the vast amounts of information transmitted through the Internet. This "world," which has no physical boundaries, is called **cyberspace**.

The benefits of the Internet are known to just about everyone who has ever needed easy and quick access to information of almost any kind. The Internet also has a darker side, however, when it comes to the exploitation of children and others who are less capable of defending themselves. People who exploit children on the Internet may be thousands of miles away from their victims. They can commit their crimes without ever showing who they really are.

So who are these **predators**, and what do they do? Most of them are **pedophiles**—people who have a sexual interest in children. In the real world, pedophiles may abuse children by forcing them to have sex. In cyberspace, they can find and look at sexual images of children. In some cases, they make their own images and share them with other pedophiles. Other people sell images to make money. These images are called child **pornography**, or porn for short. Child porn ranges from photos of nudity to videos showing terrible abuse. It is a federal crime to produce, show, or own such images. Unfortunately, however, the Internet has given open access to child porn both to pedophiles and to those who make money selling it.

The Growing Threat

As the Internet continues to expand, online predators find new ways to exploit children—and the people who produce child

Marshall Co Public L
@ Benton
1003 Poplar Stre
Benton, KY 420

BEFORE THE INTERNET

Pornography is material showing or describing sex acts. It existed in other forms long before the Internet. First there were drawings and writings. Then, after photography was invented in the 1800s, people began to print and sell pornographic photographs. There were no laws to protect the young victims of child pornography.

During the 1960s and 1970s, the amount of child porn grew. Hundreds of magazines showed pornographic photos of children. Obscene films using child victims were sold secretly around the country. Finally, in 1978, the United States passed a law that banned the use of children under 16 in pornographic photos and movies. In 1984, the law was changed to protect children under 18 years old.

For a while, these laws helped the FBI and other agencies crack down on child porn. It became harder for porn buyers and porn sellers to hide from the law. As Brad Russ, whose expert team trains FBI agents to investigate online child porn, said:

> In that day and age [the 1980s and early 1990s], it was a lot harder to distribute child pornography.

The arrival of the Internet changed all that. Although the Internet did not become widely used for personal and commercial purposes until the 1990s, several new laws have addressed online child pornography since 1988. But the laws are hard to enforce because cyber criminals are so difficult to find.

spread child porn have several ways of reaching their audience. A *New York Times* article in December 2005 explains why Internet child porn continues to grow:

> The sudden bounty of child pornography online did nothing to sate [satisfy] the desire of pedophiles. Instead, supply fueled a demand for more, for better, for more explicit—and videos replaced still pictures.

Another threat to children has emerged with the growth of the Internet. Pedophiles can easily use the Internet to make contact with children. They can reach children without parents ever knowing. Pedophiles can persuade children to send images of themselves, using email or webcams. They can persuade their victims to meet them face-to-face. If they succeed, pedophiles can then abuse children, kidnap them, or use them to make child porn.

Social Networks and Chat Rooms

Over the years, pedophiles have gained easier access to children. First

Young people enjoy using the Internet to socialize on sites like MySpace and Facebook. However, the Internet has also provided a place for pedophiles to exchange child pornography. Some predators use social networking sites to lure unsuspecting youngsters into potentially dangerous relationships.

there were online chat rooms, where people use their computers to have "conversations." More recently, social networks have boomed. Million of teens, and even younger children, have joined networking sites such as MySpace and Facebook. They post personal information and photos of themselves on the Internet.

FAST FACTS

Between 1996 and 2007, the FBI's Innocent Images unit opened more than 20,000 cases. Almost 7,000 sexual predators were convicted in that time.

The FBI fears that growing numbers of predators are using social networks to contact children. In a process known as "grooming," pedophiles encourage victims to trust them. They build friendships that can lead to opportunities for abuse.

Innocent Images

The FBI has a firm commitment to protect children from abuse. The agency leads the U.S. effort against online predators. The FBI's Cyber Crimes team works with partners across the country and abroad to find people who use the Internet to prey on children.

The FBI's most important effort against online abusers is Innocent Images. The program began in 1995. Since that time, FBI agents and their partners in local law enforcement have found and arrested thousands of pedophiles and other exploiters of children.

The job of the Innocent Images team is a difficult one. With investigators focusing on tracking them down, the criminals find more ways to hide. Michael Mason, executive assistant director of the FBI, spoke to Congress about the FBI's work in October 2007. He said:

> With heightened scrutiny in the United States, child pornographers are going further underground, using file-sharing networks and encrypted websites. They are concealing their financial mechanisms through a maze of online payment services, including the use of stolen credit cards. They are traveling to foreign countries to exploit minors. They are victimizing more children, in more ways, at younger and younger ages.

Tracking the Predators

So how do agents hunt down these invisible criminals? The FBI and its partners use a lot of **undercover** operations. Going undercover means pretending to be someone else— either a criminal or a possible victim—to set a trap for the

This equipment is part of a **database** system that stores thousands of images taken from child pornography sites. It is used by the Child Victim Identification Program to help law enforcement officers identify and help children who have been exploited by child pornographers.

real criminal. Every day, agents are working undercover online, trying to identify child abusers.

Meanwhile, FBI computer experts are working to convict these criminals. The FBI has Computer Analysis Response Teams (CARTs) at its field offices around the nation to help agents collect and analyze evidence. They collect **forensic** evidence (material that can be used in law courts) from computers and other digital equipment. In many cities, Regional Computer Forensic Laboratories (RCFLs) provide services and training to law enforcement agencies. The units seize, collect, and examine

GOING UNDERCOVER

Cyberspace provides cover for criminals, and it can provide cover for agents, too. The FBI has used false identities in several undercover operations to gain evidence of a crime. Agents can join online conversations in chat rooms used by teenagers and pre-teens. The FBI knows that predators use these chat rooms to find victims. So agents pretend to be children. Sooner or later, a pedophile will try to arrange a meeting. But instead of finding a child, the prospective abuser will find himself arrested.

Abusers are learning to be more careful. They often ask children to use webcams to prove they are in fact children. So FBI agents are going undercover in online porn networks whose members are pedophiles in search of porn. These peer-to-peer networks and eGroups offer pedophiles ways to share pornography online. Agents pretend to be pedophiles in search of child porn. They join the groups using false identities. Then they are able to gain evidence to identify the other users.

Law enforcement officers from Maryland watch as an undercover operation takes place online. Federal, state, and local agencies have had to change their tactics to keep up with online predators who are on the lookout for traps such as the one unfolding here.

In this photo, hundreds of home videos are being copied for use as evidence in the prosecution of a child pornography and prostitution ring in Illinois. In this case, a 13-year-old victim came to the authorities and led them to a home containing a huge collection of homemade child pornography.

digital evidence from computers, cameras, and cell phones. In 2007 alone, CART reported, it processed more than 2.5 million gigabytes of data for investigators.

Networks and EGroups

In 2003, the FBI began two new programs targeting online predators. Operation Peer Pressure targets child porn networks that use peer-to-peer (P2P) technology. P2P networks are file-sharing programs that enable people to access files on other users' computers. With a P2P, one pedophile can allow many other pedophiles to download his collection of porn. In the first Peer Pressure operation, agents downloaded child porn in 166 separate sessions. From these sessions, they managed to trace and find more than 100 criminals. The FBI seized computers and other evidence from the predators' homes. Since 2003, Operation Peer Pressure has continued to uncover pedophiles.

Through the operation, agents have found child molesters as well as pornographers.

An eGroup is another kind of online network. Each eGroup has a Web site where members can put messages, photos, and videos. Members can also send emails to all other members. EGroups are private, and people need a password to gain access to them. Because of this, criminals can keep their porn-sharing activities secret. Starting in 2003, FBI agents began to access eGroups trading in child porn. By 2006—the most recent year for which figures are available—they had traced and charged more than 160 people through eGroups.

FAST FACTS

Anyone who suspects online abuse of children can easily report it. The FBI has a web page at https://tips.fbi.gov/ where you can type in and send information about any crime.

Getting the Message Out

The FBI investigates crimes, but it also works to get the message out to prevent crimes. FBI agents talk to people in their communities. They teach children and parents about the dangers lurking on the Internet. The FBI Web site and those of its partners offer lots of information about staying safe online.

With the Endangered Child Alert Program, the FBI goes even farther to protect or rescue child victims. When adult faces appear in child porn photos or videos, the FBI displays those faces on its Web site. If nobody calls in to identify the criminal, the FBI will broadcast the face on national television

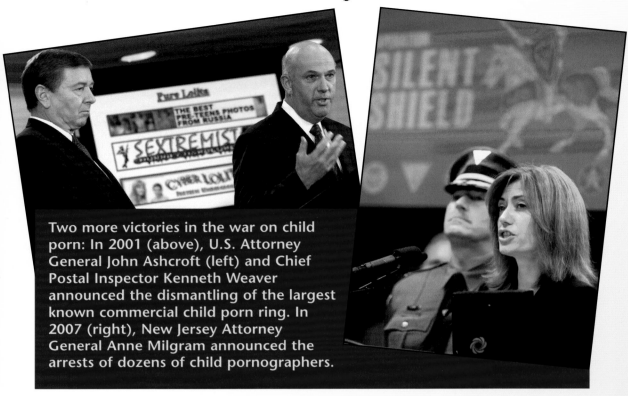

Two more victories in the war on child porn: In 2001 (above), U.S. Attorney General John Ashcroft (left) and Chief Postal Inspector Kenneth Weaver announced the dismantling of the largest known commercial child porn ring. In 2007 (right), New Jersey Attorney General Anne Milgram announced the arrests of dozens of child pornographers.

in the show *America's Most Wanted*. The first two times this happened, in February 2004, people responded right away. One woman recognized her brother and alerted her family. The child abuser was confronted by his mother and turned himself in to the sheriff's department. The FBI's Cyber Assistant Director Jana Monroe said,

> This is a shining example of how law enforcement investigations should work—a collaborative effort involving multiple law enforcement agencies together with a diligent and alert public.

Worldwide Task Force

In cyberspace, there are no national boundaries. It is just as easy to send pornography across the world as it is to send it across the street. Child abusers take full advantage of this access. Since 2004, the FBI has responded to this international problem through its Innocent Images Task Force.

"Child pornography is a global threat that requires a global response," says the FBI's assistant executive director Michael Mason. "We have no choice but to work together." The task force includes law enforcement officers from more than 20 countries. Many of them come to the United States to work with the Innocent Images unit for several months. Then they return to their own countries to continue their work as active members of the task force.

In 2008, the FBI announced it had busted a big international porn ring. The ring had its own secret Web site where pedophiles shared thousands of pornographic images of children. Twenty-two men were arrested in four countries: the United States, Germany, Australia, and Britain. Task force members and their partners also rescued about 20 children during the operation.

In this September 20, 2008, photo, FBI agents and other law enforcement officers gather at the head-quarters of an Arkansas evangelist who was the target of a child porn and sexual abuse investigation. The man was eventually charged with trans-porting young girls across state lines for sex—a federal crime that requires the par-ticipation of the FBI.

CHAPTER 4 America's Missing: Abducted Children

In the United States every year, almost 800,000 children are reported missing. That's an average of more than 2,000 children a day. About one-third of these children are abducted, which means taken by force or kidnapped.

Family Abduction

When you think of a kidnapping, you probably picture someone taken and held by a stranger. Maybe a child is taken for ransom money or because the kidnapper is an abuser. But most abducted children—about 200,000 a year—are taken by a

People in Boston, Massachusetts (top), and Tallahassee, Florida (bottom), gather to observe each state's Missing Children's Day. Showing missing children's pictures is a way of publicizing the cases and aiding in the efforts to solve them. It also puts faces to the names, adding an important human side to each case.

family member, usually a parent. They are almost always taken because of a fight over custody when parents do not live together. Custody is the right a parent has to care for and protect a child. Usually parents share custody of their children, but sometimes one parent has sole custody when that right is taken away from the other parent.

Most family abductions quickly get resolved one way or another. The children are located or returned within a few days. There is no need for the FBI to get involved. But a small number of family abductions do become FBI cases. A parent with no custody rights may take extreme steps to keep a child. Parents will sometimes flee to another state, or even another country.

Stepping In

Several U.S. laws help the FBI pursue parents who abduct children. One law concerns a parent's unlawful flight (running away from the law) to avoid prosecution. The other law says it is a crime for a parent without sole custody to take a child under 16 years old out of the country. A parent who takes a child can be arrested and charged under either of these federal laws.

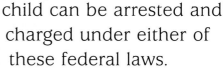

Most missing children's cases are the result of custody battles between divorced or separated parents. Fortunately, these are usually resolved quickly. Some of these cases, however, involve transporting children from one state to another or other federal crimes, and the FBI must be called in.

31

If local sheriffs or police suspect a parent has fled out of state with a child, they can ask for FBI help. The FBI can then access its many resources. The Federal Parent Locator Service (FPLS) is part of the U.S. Department of Health and Human Services. It was set up to locate parents who need to pay child support. But the FBI can also use the FPLS registry to find data on parents who abduct their children, such as their address, their employer, or their criminal history.

FAST FACTS

More than 94,000 law enforcement agency computers in the United States and Canada can access the FBI's National Crime Information Center (NCIC). The network processes about 4.8 million queries every day. The average time it takes to process a query is 0.06 seconds.

Using the NCIC

The FBI runs a huge network of data called the National Crime Information Center (NCIC). The information comes in from thousands of federal agencies and local law enforcement centers. When crimes are committed and arrest warrants issued, the data must be entered into the NCIC. Reports of missing children must be entered right away, even if there is no suspected crime.

The NCIC is a crucial tool for agents investigating child abduction. The network can offer clues to a person's location.

For example, many people who are running away with a kidnapped child will drive too fast and may be stopped for speeding. An article about abduction in the FBI *Law Enforcement Bulletin* of July 2007 explains how an NCIC search helped find an abducted child:

> When the mother did not return as scheduled, a child protective services worker made a police report. Officers had no idea which way the woman would go. An [NCIC] search revealed that an officer in Missouri had stopped her for a traffic violation only a few hours after she had picked up the child for the visit, prior to the Indianapolis [Indiana] police receiving the report of the missing child. Through a variety of tools, including federal assistance agencies, the Indianapolis investigator tracked the woman to Long Beach, California, where detectives located the suspect and her children living in a van under a bridge.

Disappeared

Not all parent abductors are caught. Some abductions are well planned, and the parent just disappears with the child, without leaving any traces. Abductors will change the names and even the appearances of themselves and their children. They will forbid their children to tell anyone about their past.

Some children have been missing for many years. The FBI maintains a Web site showing pictures and details of abductors and their victims. The photos may also appear on milk cartons and other products. They are posted in stores. One

IMAGE AGING

Sadly, some of the FBI's abduction cases are years old—and the longer children are missing, the more they will change. So how can you show what a missing child would look like after five or six years? In the FBI's crime lab, there is a team that specializes in facial age progression. This computer technique involves taking an old photograph of a person and changing it to show what they probably look like today.

There are several factors that affect how a face ages. Shared family features are important, so forensic artists use images of parents and siblings at around the same age as the abducted person. They also alter the photo to reflect aging processes that everyone shares. Eyes are larger and rounder in young children than in teenagers, for example. One more factor is the quality that makes a person different from others. Glenn Miller is the forensic imaging supervisor at the National Center for Missing and Exploited Children (NCMEC). He calls this factor "unique genetic likeness." Miller explains:

> This quality is by far the most important aspect in age-progression technology. . . . It has to do with the way the eyes, nose, and mouth relate to each other. . . . If the artist fails to preserve this relationship then the final image will be of little value.

The FBI and the NCMEC both use image aging to find missing children. The FBI also uses it to age photos of criminals who have been wanted for many years.

The pictures shown here are taken from a flyer asking for help in the return of Asha Degree, who has been missing since February 14, 2000. On the left is a photo taken of Asha at the age of nine. On the right is a picture using image aging technology to project her appearance at the age of 11.

Asha Jaquilla Degree

Photograph taken at age 9   Photograph age progressed to 11 years

day, the FBI hopes, someone will recognize a missing child.

When a parent flees the country with a child, the FBI is faced with other problems. The FBI has no right to investigate crimes or make arrests outside the United States. But it can work with law enforcers abroad. All over the world, the FBI has Legal Attaché offices (*Legats* for short). The Legats and other smaller FBI offices cover more than 200 countries, territories, and islands in other parts of the world.

FBI agents in these overseas offices follow international leads for their colleagues back in the United States. To do this, they form partnerships with local authorities and with Interpol, an international police force.

Agents (their faces digitally altered to protect their identities) arrest a suspected pedophile in Union City, New Jersey. The Bureau raided the suspect's apartment in response to a request by Interpol, the international police organization that often cooperates with the FBI and other U.S. agencies. The suspect had been the object of an international manhunt.

Cult Captives

Some children are held captive by their families without ever actually being abducted. Over the years, the FBI has become involved in a few cases that involve the children of **cult** followers. Cult followers are people who join groups or sects with extreme beliefs that separate members from the rest of society. The groups tend to form around a religion. They usually have a very strong leader who controls the members.

JONESTOWN

The People's Temple was led by a man named Jim Jones. Hundreds of followers went with Jones from the United States to Guyana in South America. There, in the jungle, they formed a settlement called Jonestown. On November 14, 1978, Congressman Leo Ryan went to visit Jonestown because he was worried about the way people there were being treated. Many of them came from his home state of California.

Ryan and other government officials talked to many people at Jonestown. Some families and individuals wanted to return to the United States with Ryan. A few days later, Ryan was at the airport, preparing to leave with several people who asked to come with him. Armed men from Jonestown started shooting at the departing group. They killed Ryan and several others.

Back at the compound, even worse things were happening. Jones persuaded the rest of his followers to drink poison. Before long, 900 people, including more than 200 children, were dead.

The FBI's Disaster Squad brought a fingerprint team and other forensic experts to Guyana. Agents interviewed the few survivors and also spoke to People's Temple followers back in the United States. The FBI was able to capture Larry Layton, who had led the shootings at the airport. Jones had already been found dead at the compound.

Cult members often form their own communities in closed compounds. They cut themselves—and their children—off from the outside world.

In 2008, the FBI took part in investigations into a sect in Texas. The sect is called the Fundamentalist Church of Jesus Christ of Latter Day Saints (FLDS). It is led by polygamists, who are people married to more than person at the same time. The males in the community under investigation had many wives, and several of these wives appeared to be underage.

Child welfare officials say a family shelter in San Angelo, Texas, received calls from a 16-year-old girl. On April 10, 2008, the *Dallas Morning News* reported the following story:

During multiple calls to the shelter's crisis hotline—the first lasting forty-two minutes—"Sarah" expressed fear of the outside world and the punishment she would receive if caught trying to escape. She also detailed sexual and physical abuse she had suffered at the hands of her fifty-year-old husband, who had fathered her child.

FBI agents and other law enforcers removed more than 450 children from the sect's compound. It was the biggest child welfare operation in U.S. history. The Texas courts ruled in May 2008 that most of the children were not in danger and had to be returned. But the State of Texas pursued charges against adult male members of the FLDS sect.

Law enforcement officers stand watch over some of the women and children who were removed from a compound belonging to a religious sect near Eldorado, Texas. FBI and other officers removed hundreds of children in response to reports of sexual abuse by male members of the sect.

CHAPTER 5

Neighborhood Nightmares: Kidnappers and Sex Offenders

Every year, thousands of children are taken by people outside their families. Officials think the number of these abductions is about 58,000 per year.

Snatched by a Stranger

Only about 12,000 of the children involved in non-family abductions are reported missing each year. Most of them, more than 90 percent, return home safely within 24 hours. But a small number of the children who disappear every year are kidnapped and not returned. Officials call these "**stereotypical** kidnappings." This is how a stereotypical kidnapping is defined by the U.S. Department of Justice:

> A nonfamily abduction perpetrated by a slight acquaintance or stranger in which a child is detained overnight, transported at least 50 miles, held for ransom or abducted with intent to keep the child permanently, or killed.

These are the kidnappings we see reported on television. They are the terrible stories that make people afraid for their children's safety. But official figures show that only 115 cases out of the annual 58,000 fit this description.

The Offenders

As the last chapter showed, most abductors are family members. The Department of Justice separates other kidnappers into two groups. About half are strangers to the victim. The rest are known—however slightly—to the victim.

Whether they are strangers or family friends, many people who abduct children will sexually abuse them. Some are young men who will rape girls close to their own age. More than half of all non-family abductions involve children aged from 15 to 17 years old. Other kidnappers are older people, also usually men, who abduct young children in order to abuse them.

The FBI's National Sex Offender Registry helps make the presence of sexual predators known to citizens and local authorities alike.

KEEPING TRACK OF SEX OFFENDERS

In 1996, a new law named the Lychner Act required that the Department of Justice set up a database of sex offenders. The FBI coordinated the creation of the National Sex Offender Registry and continues to maintain it. There are more than 400,000 names in the database. When offenders are released from prison, they are required to register their address with the FBI and with authorities in their state. If they move, they must notify the authorities again.

"Megan's Law" is the name for state laws that require information about sex offenders to be made public. The first Megan's Law was passed in New Jersey in 1994, the home state of Megan Kanka. Megan was seven years old when she was raped and murdered by a neighbor. The neighbor was a convicted sex offender. "We knew nothing about him," says Megan's mother, Maureen Kanka. "If we had been aware of his record, my daughter would be alive today."

Megan's Laws vary from state to state. Every state decides what information should be made public. Usually, offenders' names, photos, and addresses are displayed on Web sites that anyone can access. The Department of Justice also has a national sex offender Web site, which offers access to all state information. In some states, schools and daycare centers receive notices if offenders move into the area. If the offenders are considered to be a high risk, families living nearby will also be notified.

Pedophiles who are known to the FBI and other law enforcers are classified as sex **offenders**. The FBI keeps a database of these people, called the National Sex Offender Registry. The FBI also includes kidnappers and other sex offenders in its list of "Ten Most Wanted **Fugitives**."

The Lindbergh Case

A small number of kidnappings are done for money. The FBI's involvement in child abduction dates back to a famous case in the 1930s. The 20-month-old son of famed aviator Charles Lindbergh and his wife, writer Anne Morrow Lindbergh, who was also a pioneering aviator, was snatched from his room on March 1, 1932. The crime did not involve sexual abuse. The kidnapper delivered several ransom notes (written demands for money) over a period of weeks. The Lindberghs paid the ransom, but the child's dead body was found soon afterward.

U.S. President Herbert Hoover ordered the FBI to lead a federal investigation. Agents followed thousands of leads while the FBI's new crime lab analyzed the ransom notes. The FBI

FAST FACTS

The FBI's role in the Lindbergh case led to a new law. In 1932, Congress made kidnapping a federal crime. Today, if a child is kidnapped, the FBI can get involved right away.

When the son of Charles and Anne Morrow Lindbergh was kidnapped in 1932, the FBI was called into the case. The kidnapping made news all over the world. It also thrust the Bureau into the role it now plays in leading investigations of child kidnappings.

SEEN THIS BABY?

LIGHT

EYES BLUE

CHIN DEEPLY DIMPLED

WEIGHT 30 POUNDS

HEIGHT 2 FEET 9 INCHES

CHARLES A. LINDBERGH, JR.

Photo from Pathé News.

AMBER ALERT

In the most dangerous abduction cases, state law enforcers use the AMBER Alert system. AMBER is an acronym. Its letters stand for America's Missing: Broadcast Emergency Response. The goal of AMBER Alert is simple: to get the word out to as many people as possible, as quickly as possible. So when a child is abducted and in great danger, an AMBER Alert is issued. Radio broadcasters interrupt their programs to make announcements. TV shows stop for news bulletins. Highway signs show the alerts, and the message can also be sent out to cell phones.

AMBER Alerts work. They have helped save lives and locate hundreds of children. Several children have even been released after their abductors heard the alert on radio or TV.

The AMBER Alert System is named for Amber Hagerman. Amber was nine years old on January 13, 1996, when she was riding her bicycle near her home in Arlington, Texas. A man drew up in a truck, snatched Amber from her bike, and drove her away. Amber's body was found a few days later, just a few miles away from where she had been kidnapped. Her murderer was never found.

A year after Amber's death, the AMBER Alert system was created in the Dallas area. It has since grown into a nationwide program.

put together a **profile** and drawings of the kidnapper. Through long hours on the case, agents tracked the ransom money. On September 19, 1934, a tip from a gas station attendant led them to Bruno Richard Hauptmann, who was arrested and later convicted and executed for the crime.

This AMBER Alert sign appeared over a stretch of highway in Omaha, Nebraska, soon after a car with a nine-month-old baby in the back seat was stolen from a gas station. The car and the child were safely recovered several hours later.

Finding Elizabeth

In June 2002, a young girl was snatched from her bedroom in Salt Lake City, Utah. Fourteen-year-old Elizabeth Smart lived through a nine-month ordeal at the hands of her kidnappers. All the while, FBI agents and local police officers were on the trail. They were investigating several suspects when Elizabeth's younger sister voiced her own suspicion: She thought the kidnapper was a handyman who had worked at the Smart house. A drawing of him was released to the public. Within days, Elizabeth was sighted and rescued.

FAST FACTS

The FBI posts photos and information concerning missing children online at www.fbi.gov/wanted/kidnap/kidmiss.htm. People can call 911 or contact the FBI if they think that they have some information about a missing child. They can also call the National Center for Missing and Exploited Children (NCMEC) at 1-800-THE-LOST.

Chip Burrus, agent in charge of the FBI's Salt Lake City office, spoke at a news conference in March 2003, after Elizabeth was found. "We had two goals," he said. "The first one was to bring her back safely. And the second was to locate the people who did this. On both of those objectives we think we've accomplished that."

In a 2008 interview with *People* magazine, Elizabeth described what she went through. For the first three months,

Child kidnap victim Elizabeth Smart (second from left) is shown here accepting an award in 2004 for courage. Elizabeth, now a young adult, helps other children stay safe by promoting ID kits for kids. The FBI supports the National Child Identification Program, which gives away ID kits that parents can keep in case their children go missing.

she spent most of her time chained to a tree. She was sexually abused and lived mostly on bread. But Elizabeth is determined to put the nightmare behind her. "From the day I came home," she said, "I haven't wasted time looking back."

Rapid Response

The FBI created Child Abduction Rapid Deployment (CARD) teams in 2005 to provide a fast response to kidnappings. The first few hours after an abduction are the most crucial, and CARD teams work fast.

Team members are experienced in crimes against children. They also have access to FBI experts. These experts could be

The FBI urges people to take time to look at photos of missing children. This gallery of pictures appears on the FBI's Web site with the following note: ". . . just a very few of the children who are far away from home tonight."

forensic scientists, who study evidence left at crime scenes. They could be analysts who understand criminal behavior. Agents team up with state and local law enforcement. They add their skills in investigation and their federal resources to local knowledge. They alert other law enforcement agencies about missing children. As Janice Mertz, head of the FBI's Crimes Against Children unit, explains: "We want our best people moving as fast as they can and using every skill they've got to find missing kids and bring them home safely. That's the bottom line of this initiative."

6 Finding the Killers: Murders and Massacres

The FBI is often called in to deal with extremely violent crimes. Agents offer their resources and experience to state and local partners. These partners bring important local knowledge to an investigation. Together, the FBI and local law officers investigate cases in which children are murdered. Every year, about 1,800 children are victims of homicide (the legal name for the crime of killing a person).

Helping Solve Violent Crimes

The FBI's Crimes Against Children unit is part of the agency's Major Thefts and Violent Crimes division. Another FBI division is the National Center for the Analysis of Violent Crime (NCAVC). The NCAVC helps the Crimes Against Children unit solve crimes. Law offi-

The National Center for the Analysis of Violent Crime(NCAVC) is based at the FBI Academy in Quantico, Virginia. The NCAVC and its divisions, such as the Behavioral Analysis Unit, may be accessed online at the FBI's Web site.

Serial Murder

Multi-Disciplinary Perspectives for Investigators

BEHAVIORAL ANALYSIS UNIT
NATIONAL CENTER FOR THE ANALYSIS OF VIOLENT CRIME

cers can request help from the NCAVC for such crimes as child abduction, serial murders, rape, and bombings—crimes where there is a serious threat of violence. There are three parts to the NCAVC:

FAST FACTS

Over the last 15 to 20 years, violent crimes, including murders, have been slowly decreasing. The FBI reported a decrease of 1.4 percent in violent crimes from 2006 to 2007.

- The Behavioral Analysis Unit (BAU) helps investigators by examining criminal behavior.
- The Violent Crime Apprehension Program (ViCAP) maintains a database of information about violent and repeated crimes.
- The Child Abduction and Serial Murder Investigative Resources Center (CASMIRC) helps solve kidnappings and killings.

In addition to providing assistance in violent crime cases, the NCAVC also offers training to law enforcement agencies.

Understanding the Criminal Mind

The BAU helps solves crimes with what it calls "criminal investigative analysis." BAU staff members look at the crime scene and evidence. They review all the facts known about a case. Then they analyze all the information they have. The BAU may come up with a profile of the offender. This would give police or agents a good idea of the kind of person they are looking for. The BAU may also figure out the reasons

Analysis of the hand-writing and contents of this ransom note in the 1932 kidnapping of the Lindbergh baby helped the FBI create a profile of the baby's kidnapper and murderer, Bruno Richard Hauptmann.

behind the crime and advise about any future threat.

The FBI has used profiling to find criminals for many years. Back in the 1930s, investigators used a profile to track the kidnapper and killer in the Lindbergh case. In that case, they used the handwriting in the ransom notes and other evidence to build a picture of the criminal. Today, the BAU uses experts in **psychology** and criminology to create profiles.

Finding Patterns, Matching Crimes

The ViCAP database keeps track of violent crimes that remain unsolved. It reveals patterns when a crime is repeated. The program is used in many cases, especially those involving abductions and unsolved murders.

Unidentified bodies and missing people are entered in ViCAP if the FBI suspects that a crime has taken place.

ViCAP can be used to research all kinds of crimes, from child abuse to serial killings to school shootings. The FBI and other agencies use ViCAP to compare and possibly match crimes. If a pattern is found, it will often

Using methods developed by Howard Teten, the FBI was able to construct a profile that led to the arrest of David Meirhofer, the kidnapper and killer of seven-year-old Susan Jaeger (above).

FBI PROFILER

In the mid-1970s, Howard Teten was teaching criminology at the FBI. Teten studied psychology and also had years of experience as an investigator. He was able to link certain crime scenes with certain mental patterns. For example, Teten could figure out how old a criminal was by the kind of killing. He could tell if the FBI was dealing with a psychopath, a person who can commit criminal acts and not let a knowledge of right or wrong influence him or her. "A psychopath will actually kill someone and then sit where the police drink coffee and listen," says Howard Teten. "If they stop investigating, he may commit another crime to get the police going."

Teten became more and more convinced that profiling could help identify criminals. When the FBI launched its first behavioral science unit in 1972, Teten joined the team. Soon afterward, the FBI used Teten's profiling skills to find a serial killer. In June 1973, seven-year-old Susan Jaeger was snatched from her tent on a campsite in Montana. Teten and his colleagues created a profile of her abductor. They said he was a young, white, male psychopath. They sketched out behavior and character clues that led to the arrest of David Meirhofer. Investigators found Susan's body and evidence of other victims at the killer's home.

provide investigators with a lead. ViCAP also offers advice and support to investigators.

Cold Case Files

ViCAP can be used to solve cases from the past. Old, unsolved crimes are called "cold cases." They may have remained a mystery for years. The FBI has released several examples of how ViCAP helped solve cold cases, including this one:

> In 1989 investigators from Pennsylvania entered a case from 1951 into the ViCAP database. In this case, a man was found guilty of murdering a young girl. Not long after, investigators from Illinois entered an unsolved case from 1957, in which an approximately eight-year-old girl was murdered. ViCAP analysts noticed similarities in the two cases. Due to these similarities and other related evidence, detectives in Illinois were able to solve a crime that occurred almost forty years ago and finally resolve a terrible mystery for the parents.

New technology can help solve cold cases after many years. The FBI's DNA Analysis Unit uses DNA (information carried in human cells) to identify criminals and victims. This process was not available until the 1980s. But traces of a killer's DNA on a victim's body can be analyzed years later. Today, the FBI has several million DNA profiles on file. ViCAP and other FBI databases can match these profiles to DNA from crime scenes.

DNA can also be used to prove innocence. Six-year-old JonBenét Ramsey was found murdered in her home in 1996. Her killer was never found, but her parents and brother had always been suspects. A new kind of test called "touch DNA" found evidence of unknown DNA on the child's clothing that matched an earlier sample. Authorities announced in July 2008 that, together, the two DNA samples indicated that an unknown man was the killer. Cleared of suspicion, JonBenét's father was hopeful that the killer would be found. "We have a good, solid, irrefutable DNA sample," he said. "We have a good opportunity to find an answer to who did this."

John Ramsey (center), the father of JonBenét Ramsey, was cleared of suspicion in his daughter's killing by new DNA technology. HIs wife, Patsy, who was also a suspect, died of cancer in June of 2006, nearly two years before it was revealed that she, too, was no longer a suspect in her daughter's death.

Multiple Killings

Some of the worst cases the FBI deals with are multiple killings. The Child Abduction and Serial Murder Investigative Resources Center (CASMIRC) was set up in 1998. The center specializes in investigating child kidnappings, child killings, and serial murders. If any law enforcement agency in the United States is dealing with a serial killer, CASMIRC can offer help. It coordinates and provides resources from all other FBI units when a crime takes place. CASMIRC also does prevention work and offers training.

The FBI deals with other kinds of multiple killings, and some of these cases involve children. There are a few killers who try to murder as many people as possible in one terrible event. They may use a bomb to blow up a building. They may open fire with a gun in a public place.

Since the late 1990s, the FBI has investigated a number of shootings in schools. The killings were not related, and such incidents are very rare. But they cause great anxiety among parents, teachers, and children. Supervisory Special Agent Mary Ellen O'Toole works in the FBI's Behavior Analysis Unit and has written reports on school shootings. In a 2006 interview, she said, "There is no typical school shooter. They don't fall within a set of traits and characteristics." But, she says, there can be plenty of signs if people pay attention to others around them. "Be aware of people's moods," says O'Toole. "People who act out violently don't wake up one morning and snap. There are clues."

BOMBING IN BIRMINGHAM

On September 15, 1963, a bomb exploded at the Sixteenth Street Baptist Church in Birmingham, Alabama. Reporter Ronald Kessler described the event in his book, *The Bureau*:

> That day in 1963, Denise McNair, eleven, and Carole Robertson, Cynthia Wesley, and Addie Mae Collins, all fourteen, were dressed in white party dresses and patent leather shoes for a youth service. Nineteen bundled sticks of dynamite concealed under a stairwell exploded inches from them.

The girls were killed, and more than 20 other people were injured in the blast. The victims were African American, and the bombing was an act of racial hatred. FBI agents interviewed hundreds of people. They made secret voice recordings of suspects. The FBI identified four suspects, all members of the hate group the Ku Klux Klan.

In spite of the investigation, nobody was arrested at first. The tape recordings were not admissible in court and could not be used as evidence. And crucial witnesses were too scared to speak up. The FBI was criticized and accused of covering up evidence.

In 1977, the state of Alabama managed to con-

FBI agents search for clues in the 1963 bombing of a church in Birmingham, Alabama.

vict one of the men, Robert Chambliss. Herman Cash, who was considered to be one of the suspects, died in 1994 without being charged. There were still two suspects left, however. In the mid-1990s, the FBI reopened its case. The old voice tapes were enhanced using modern technology to the extent that they could be used as evidence. Witnesses, some of them too afraid to speak earlier, now came forward. In 2001, Thomas Blanton was convicted of murder. It had taken almost 38 years to bring him to justice. In 2002, Bobby Frank Cherry was also convicted.

Law enforcement officers rescue students from Columbine High School, in Littleton, Colorado, during a shooting rampage on April 20, 1999, in which 13 victims were killed. Perhaps more than any other school shooting, Columbine focused the nation's attention on such issues as guns, the climate of violence in U.S. society, and the effects of social and personal pressures on children.

Crime-Fighting Partners

Crimes against children show the worst aspects of human nature. Children cannot defend themselves against adults. People who exploit, harm, and kill children are despised for their acts. Fortunately these terrible cases are just a tiny percentage of all crimes committed. But in spite of the relatively small numbers, the FBI works constantly to find the criminals and bring them to justice. It also makes great efforts to prevent such crimes from happening at all.

Throughout its history, the FBI has supported its partners in law enforcement with training and resources. Its stated mission is "to provide leadership and criminal justice services to federal, state, municipal, and international agencies and partners." These partners are central to the Crimes Against Children unit. So is the unit's relationship with the public and media. The FBI knows that all its partnerships are crucial in its work to protect children.

The combination of computer technology and DNA analysis has helped the FBI make huge strides in its ability to identify criminal suspects.

FIGHTING CRIME WITH SCIENCE AND TECHNOLOGY

Since 1932, the FBI Laboratory has been using science to help solve crimes. The lab has matched fingerprints and examined microscopic fibers. Agents have pieced together countless fragments from crime scenes, turning them into vital evidence. The 1980s and 1990s saw a huge leap forward in crime detection. Forensic science (science used in the law) has gained many new tools. These tools help the FBI identify criminals and solve cases against them.

One major breakthrough was DNA analysis. DNA is information carried in people's cells. It can be used to link a person to a crime or to identify missing persons. Today, FBI files contain several million DNA profiles as well as millions of fingerprint sets.

Computer power helped the FBI's Criminal Justice Information Services build a huge **database**. The system handles an average of 5.5 million queries every day. Data can be used to track down criminals in several ways. One method is link analysis. A computer can pull together all kinds of information—police records, photos, phone logs, and agents' notes—and see how it connects. The FBI also has a unit called the Computer Analysis and Response Team (CART). The team's experts pull all kinds of crucial evidence from criminals' computers.

CHRONOLOGY

1932: The child of Charles and Anne Morrow Lindbergh is kidnapped and murdered in New Jersey.

Congress makes kidnapping a federal offense.

1963: A bomb explosion at the Sixteenth Street Baptist church in Birmingham, Alabama, kills four girls.

1972: The FBI launches its first behavioral science unit.

1977: Robert Chambliss is convicted of murder in the 1963 bombing of the Sixteenth Street Baptist Church in Birmingham, Alabama.

1978: The United States bans the use of minors under the age of 16 in pornography.

Nine hundred people, including more than 200 children, all followers of cult leader Jim Jones, die in Jonestown, Guyana, in a mass suicide.

1984: The National Center for the Analysis of Violent Crime (NCAVC) opens at the FBI Academy.

The United States extends ban on the use of minors in pornography to include children under 18.

1994: The FBI's Critical Incident Response Group is formed.

The first Megan's Law, requiring that states make public information about sex offenders, is passed in New Jersey.

Herman Cash, considered a suspect in the bombing of the Sixteenth Street Baptist

Church in Birmingham, Alabama, in 1963, dies before charges are issued against him.

1995: FBI's Operation Innocent Images, targeting Internet-based child pornography, begins.

1996: Lychner Act requires Department of Justice to set up a database of sex offenders.

JonBenét Ramsey is found murdered in her home in Boulder, Colorado. Her parents, at one time considered suspects in her killing, are cleared of suspicion in part due to advanced DNA technology, 12 years later.

1997: AMBER Alert system is established in Texas.

1998: FBI's Child Abduction and Serial Murder Investigative Resources Center (CASMIRC) is established.

1999: Two students at Columbine High School in Littleton, Colorado, go on a shooting rampage, killing 12 students and one teacher before killing themselves. The episode focused attention on various children's issues and sparked a national debate over the availability of guns and the culture of violence in entertainment, especially for children.

2001: Thomas Blanton is convicted of murder for the 1963 bombing at Sixteenth Street Baptist Church in Birmingham, Alabama.

Bobby Frank Cherry is convicted for the same crime the following year.

2002: Elizabeth Smart is kidnapped in June.

Shawn Hornbeck is kidnapped in October.

Bobby Frank Cherry is convicted of the 1963 murder of four girls at the Sixteenth Street Baptist Church in Birmingham, Alabama.

The murder of a child in Oklahoma City, Oklahoma, sparks a national FBI investigation of child prostitution.

2003: The FBI's Innocence Lost program and Operation Peer Pressure begin.

Elizabeth Smart is rescued from her kidnappers.

2004: Innocent Images unit establishes international task force.

The FBI turns to a television show, *America's Most Wanted*, to capture two men who appeared in pornography that featured abused children.

2005: The FBI begins its Human Trafficking Initiative.

Operation Precious Cargo, targeting a large prostitution ring, concludes successfully in December.

Child Abduction Rapid Deployment (CARD) teams are created within the FBI.

2007: Ben Ownby is kidnapped on January 8 and rescued along with Shawn Hornbeck on January 12.

The FBI opens 120 investigations into human trafficking that result in 155 arrests.

2008: Operation Cross Country results in the arrest of more than 350 people in connection with child trafficking or other forms of child exploitation.

The Innocent Images international task force and its partners arrest members of an international child pornography ring.

FBI agents and other law enforcement officers remove more than 450 children from the compound of a religious sect in Texas.

DNA evidence clears the family of JonBenét Ramsey of her murder after 12 years.

GLOSSARY

abduction—the act of taking someone away by force or of taking and keeping a child without the right of custody.

abuse—unfair or cruel treatment.

analyze—carefully study information or an object to find out the truth about it. An analyst is someone who examines (analyzes) information or objects professionally.

cult—a group of people, usually small and often organized around a central figure having a strong influence on the group, that is devoted to particular beliefs that are not in the mainstream of thinking in the society as a whole.

cyberspace—not a "space" in the usual sense, but the environment created on computers by all of the information and systems that are available over the Internet.

database—a large, organized collection of information stored in a computer system.

evidence—material used to uncover truth or to prove guilt.

exploitation—the act of unfairly using or taking advantage of someone.

federal—national or relating to the whole nation.

forensic—relating to or suitable to use in law courts. Forensic science or evidence can be used to prove a criminal's guilt.

fugitive—a person who is running away, especially someone who is trying to escape from the law.

offender—a person who commits an offense or a crime.

pedophile—a person who has a sexual interest in young children.

pornography—writings or images that describe or show sex acts.

predator—a person who preys on (devours or destroys) others like an animal; often used to describe adults who go to great lengths to find children to abuse or harm.

profile—a collection of information about a person—such as descriptions of character or DNA—that can be used to help find or identify a criminal.

prostitution—the exchange of sexual services for something else, usually money.

psychology—study of the mind and human behavior.

stereotypical—fitting a common idea of how things are. A stereotypical kidnapping is one that fits the popular image of a kidnapping, even though other types of kidnappings are actually much more common.

sweatshop—a factory or workshop, usually in the clothing or textile industry, where people are forced to work under poor conditions at jobs that pay little or nothing.

task force—a team put together for a particular job, or task.

undercover—disguised in order to gain entry into criminal circles.

vulnerable—easily harmed or likely to be in danger.

FURTHER READING

Crewe, Sabrina. *A History of the FBI*. Broomall, PA: Mason Crest Publishers, 2009.

De Capua, Sarah. *The FBI*. New York: Children's Press, 2007.

De Hahn, Tracee. *Crimes Against Children: Child Abuse and Neglect*. New York: Chelsea House Publishers, 1999.

Grayson, Robert. *The FBI and Cyber Crimes*. Broomall, PA: Mason Crest Publishers, 2009.

Holden, Henry M. *FBI 100 Years: An Unofficial History*. Minneapolis: Zenith Press, 2008.

Theoharis, Athan G., editor. *The FBI: A Comprehensive Reference Guide*. New York: Checkmark Books, 2000.

INTERNET RESOURCES

http://www.fbi.gov/fbikids.htm
The kids' page of the official FBI Web site provides activities and information about the FBI for 6th grade to 12th grade students.

http://www.fbi-sos.org/
This safe Web site for online surfing was developed at the Miami FBI field office.

http://www.idthecreep.com/
You think you know who is emailing, chatting, or IM'ing with you? Play "ID the Creep," and see how you score when it comes to picking out the bad from the good.

http://www.missingkids.com/
Web site of the National Center for Missing and Exploited Children (NCMEC) offers information about missing children, safety tips for kids and parents, and links for reporting sightings and other tips.

http://tcs.cybertipline.com/knowthedangers.htm
Web site of the NCMEC "Don't Believe the Type" campaign has information about the online risks found in chat rooms, social networks, and bulletin boards.

> The Web sites mentioned in this book were active at the time of publication. The publisher is not responsible for Web sites that have changed their addresses or discontinued operation since the date of publication. The publisher will review and update the Web site addresses each time the book is reprinted.

NOTES

Chapter 1

p. 7: "What a blessing . . ." Roland J. Corvington, quoted in "Working Together—Bringing Two Teens Home," Federal Bureau of Investigation, February 16, 2007, http://www.fbi.gov/page2/feb07/missingteens021607.htm.

p. 7: "There's no way . . ." Craig Akers, quoted in Betsy Taylor, "Abducted Boy Marks 1st Anniversary Home," *USA Today*, January 11, 2008, http://www.usatoday.com/news/nation/2008-01-11-4146365967_x.htm.

p. 8: "You try not to worry . . ." Don Ownby, interviewed on *Today*, NBC Television, January 8, 2008.

p. 10: "Our nation has made . . ." George W. Bush, speech at Presidential Hall, Dwight D. Eisenhower Executive Office Building, Washington, D.C., October 23, 2002.

Chapter 2

p. 15: "1.6 million children . . ." Chris Swecker, statement before the Commission on Security and Cooperation in Europe, United States Helsinki Commission, Washington, D.C., June 7, 2005.

p. 15: "Thousands of young girls . . ." Bay Fang, "Young Lives for Sale," *U.S. News and World Report*, October 24, 2005, http://www.usnews.com/usnews/news/articles/051024/24sextraffickers.htm.

p. 16: "For cases involving . . ." Jamie Konstas, quoted in "Up Close and Personal—Intelligence Analyst Works to Save Kids," Federal Bureau of Investigation, July 14, 2006, http://www.fbi.gov/page2/july06/career_konstas071406.htm.

p. 17: "The more we looked . . ." Mike Beaver, quoted in Bay Fang, "Young Lives for Sale."

Chapter 3

p. 21: "In that day and age . . ." Brad Russ, quoted in Eichenwald, "A Shadowy Trade Migrates to the Web."

p. 22: "The sudden bounty of . . ." Kurt Eichenwald, "A Shadowy Trade Migrates to the Web," *New York Times*, December 19, 2005, http://www.nytimes.com/2005/12/19/business/19kidswebhistory.html.

p. 24: "With heightened security . . ." Michael A. Mason, statement before the Committee on House Judiciary, Washington, D.C., October 17, 2007.

p. 28: "This is a shining example . . ." Jana Monroe, quoted in "A Strengthened Partnership: Name That Sexual Predator!" Federal Bureau of Investigation, March 3, 2004, http://www.fbi.gov/page2/march04/predator030304.htm.

p. 29: "Child pornography is . . ." Mason, statement before the Committee on House Judiciary, October 17, 2007.

Chapter 4

p. 33: "When the mother . . ." David M. Allender, "Child Abductions: Nightmares in Progress," *FBI Law Enforcement Bulletin*, July 2007, http://findarticles.com/p/articles/mi_m2194/is_/ai_n27325842.

p. 34: "This quality is by far . . ." Glenn Miller, "The Lost Children," *Secrets of the Face, New Scientist*, October 2, 2004, volume 284, issue 2467, pp. 12–13.

p. 37: "During multiple calls . . ." Emily Ramshaw and Paul Meyer, "CPS Says Teen Who Reported Polygamist Ranch Is Probably in Its Care," *Dallas Morning News*, April 10, 2008, http://www.dallasnews.com/sharedcontent/dws/news/texassouthwest/stories/DNpolygamists_10tex.ART.State.Edition1.46ab4b7.html.

Chapter 5

p. 38: "A nonfamily abduction . . ." David Finkelhor, Heather Hammer, and Andrea J. Sedlak, "Nonfamily Abducted Children: National Estimates and Characteristics," *National Incidence Studies of Missing, Abducted, Runaway, and Thrownaway Children*, U.S. Department of Justice, October 2002.

p. 40: "We knew nothing about him . . ." Maureen Kanka, quoted in "Our Mission," Megan Nicole Kanka Foundation, Inc., http://www.megannicolekankafoundation.org/mission.htm.

p. 43: "We had two goals . . . " Chris Burrus, quoted in Dean E. Murphy, "Utah Girl's Family Sees Polygamy as a Possible Motive," *New York Times*, March 14, 2003, p. A1, http://proquest.umi.com/pqdweb?did=305621411&Fmt=3&clientld=63553&RQT=309&VName=PQD.

p. 44: "From the day I came . . ." Elizabeth Smart, quoted in Cathy Free, Alex Tresniowski,

"A Second Chance at Life," *People*, June 23, 2008, http://www.people.com/people/archive/article/0,,20207194,00.html.

p. 45: "We want our best people . . ." Janice Mertz, quoted in "When Kids Go Missing—Our New Team Will Help Find Them," Federal Bureau of Investigation, June 16, 2006, http://www.fbi.gov/page2/june06/card_teams061606.htm.

Chapter 6

p. 49: "A psychopath will actually kill . . ." Howard Teten, quoted in Ronald Kessler, *The Bureau: The Secret History of the FBI* (New York: St. Martin's Paperbacks, 2003), p. 272.

p. 50: "In 1989 investigators from . . ." National Center for the Analysis of Violent Crime, Federal Bureau of Investigation, http://www.fbi.gov/hq/isd/cirg/ncavc.htm.

p. 51: "We have a good, solid . . ." John Ramsey, quoted in DeeDee Correll, "JonBenet Ramsey's Family Cleared in Child's 1996 Slaying," *Los Angeles Times*, July 10, 2008, http://articles.latimes.com/2008/jul/10/nation/na-jonbenet10.

p. 52: "There is no typical . . .", Mary Ellen O'Toole, quoted in "School Shootings—What You Should Know," Federal Bureau of Investigation, October 6, 2006, http://www.fbi.gov/page2/oct2006/schoolshootings100606.htm.

p. 53: "That day in 1963 . . ." Kessler, p. 428.

p. 55: "To provide leadership . . ." Our Mission, Federal Bureau of Investigation, http://www.fbi.gov/quickfacts.htm.

INDEX

About the Author

Sabrina Crewe is an editor of children's educational books. She has edited many series of social studies and science books and is the author or co-author of 50 titles, including two in this series.